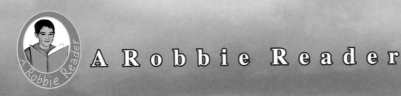

A Robbie Reader

What's So Great About . . . ?

THE BUFFALO SOLDIERS

Tamra Orr

Mitchell Lane
PUBLISHERS

P.O. Box 196
Hockessin, Delaware 19707
Visit us on the web: www.mitchelllane.com
Comments? email us: mitchelllane@mitchelllane.com

Mitchell Lane
PUBLISHERS

Printing   1   2   3   4   5   6   7   8   9

A Robbie Reader
What's So Great About . . . ?

Amelia Earhart	Anne Frank	Annie Oakley
Barack Obama	**The Buffalo Soldiers**	Christopher Columbus
Daniel Boone	Davy Crockett	The Donner Party
Elizabeth Blackwell	Ferdinand Magellan	Francis Scott Key
Galileo	George Washington Carver	Harriet Tubman
Helen Keller	Henry Hudson	Jacques Cartier
Johnny Appleseed	King Tut	Lewis and Clark
Martin Luther King Jr.	Michelle Obama	Paul Bunyan
Pocahontas	Robert Fulton	Rosa Parks
Sam Houston	The Tuskegee Airmen	

Library of Congress Cataloging-in-Publication Data
Orr, Tamra.
  What's so great about the Buffalo Soldiers / by Tamra Orr.
     p. cm. — (A Robbie reader) (What's so great about ... ?)
  Includes bibliographical references and index.
  ISBN 978-1-58415-831-8 (library bound)
  1. United States. Army—African American troops—History--Juvenile literature. 2. African American soldiers—History—Juvenile literature. I. Title.
  E185.63.O77 2010
  355.008996073—dc22
                                                                                    2009027361

ABOUT THE AUTHOR: Tamra Orr has written nearly 200 nonfiction books for readers of all ages, including *What's So Great About the Tuskegee Airmen?* for Mitchell Lane Publishers. She graduated from Ball State University in Indiana with a degree in English and Secondary Education. Now she lives in the Pacific Northwest with her four kids, husband, dog, and cat.

PUBLISHER'S NOTE: The following story has been thoroughly researched and to the best of our knowledge represents a true story. While every possible effort has been made to ensure accuracy, the publisher will not assume liability for damages caused by inaccuracies in the data, and makes no warranty on the accuracy of the information contained herein.

TABLE OF CONTENTS

Words in **bold** type can be found in the glossary.

The 9th Cavalry Regiment included two future Medal of Honor recipients: George Jordan, seated third from left, and Henry Johnson, standing to the left of the flag.

A Cry for Help

The long day, May 13, 1880, had finally ended. The twenty-five men from the 9th **Cavalry** were exhausted. They were on their way to Fort Tularosa and had traveled many miles. Each one, including leader Sergeant George Jordan, was looking forward to taking off his boots, eating a hot meal, and heading off to sleep.

That changed when a messenger came into their camp in southwestern New Mexico. He was scared and needed help right away. Fort Tularosa, a small **community** (kuh-MYOO-nih-tee) of families, was in danger. The Apache leader Victorio, known as "The Triumphant One," was coming fast! If he reached the fort, he would kill everyone there. If the soldiers of the 9th Cavalry did not arrive before Victorio, the families would be doomed.

To help these people, the cavalrymen (KAV-ul-ree-men) would have to give up sleeping in their warm blankets. They would have to march all night through the cold mountains—their horses were too tired to make the trip. When Jordan asked them what they wanted to do, however, these brave soldiers did not think twice. They pulled their boots back on. After a quick bite to eat, they headed out into the darkness.

As the sun rose the next morning, the 9th Cavalry arrived at the fort. Were they too late? They were relieved when grateful families poured out of their homes to welcome them.

The men spent the day repairing buildings

Victorio was soft-spoken in person, but he was also known to be fierce in battle.

and making the fort stronger. They finished just in time. Victorio attacked that night, but the fighting was over quickly. When the dust settled, Victorio and his 100 warriors had run off. The twenty-five soldiers

Some of the men who helped protect the settlers from Victorio were Sergeant Nathan Fletcher (top left) and Robert Burley (bottom, second from left).

in Jordan's **detachment** (dee-TATCH-ment) had won. Not a single person or animal from Tularosa was lost in the battle. Ten years later, Jordan would be given a Medal of Honor for his bravery at this battle.

As Jordan looked around at his men, he smiled. Protecting the settlers on the plains, without complaint and with bravery, was what these soldiers were all about. He was proud to be one of them.

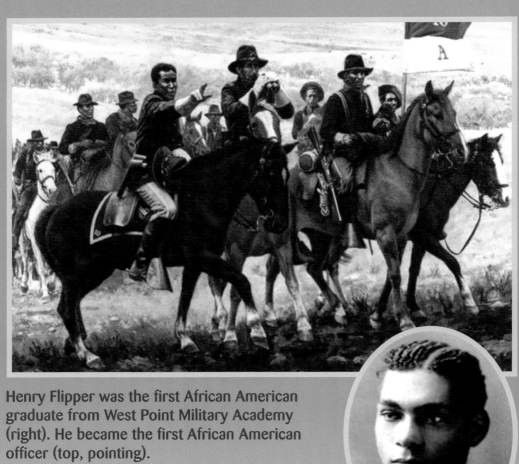

Henry Flipper was the first African American graduate from West Point Military Academy (right). He became the first African American officer (top, pointing).

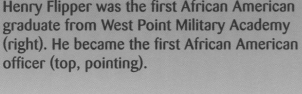

A Long History

The Buffalo Soldiers were all-black **regiments** (REH-juh-munts) of the U.S. Army. Formed in 1866, they were charged with keeping peace between settlers and the Native Americans who already lived on the **frontier.**

These soldiers were not the first blacks to fight for the United States of America. During the Revolutionary War (1775–1783), more than 7,000 African American soldiers fought for the country's independence.

During the War of 1812 between the United States and Great Britain, blacks played a role in several key battles. When the North and South sides of the country fought the Civil War (1861–1865), 186,000 African Americans joined the battle for the Union. These were the United States Colored Troops. More than

33,000 of these troops were killed. Every time the nation has faced a battle, blacks have been there, sharing their courage and determination.

When the Civil War ended, Congress passed Bill #138, which created a new kind of military. The country would organize a troop of soldiers who were not ordered to win wars. Instead, they would work during peacetime.

Bill #138 set up six regiments of black troops. Four were **infantry,** or foot soldiers. The other two were cavalry, or on horseback. They were given the oldest rifles, the most aged horses, and the wettest, coldest, most unpleasant **quarters.** All were commanded by white leaders, because many white people thought blacks were not capable of being in charge. Even brave George Jordan was under Captain Charles Parker, who was white.

These troops did not have to face the enemy on the front lines, but they still had a dangerous and difficult mission. Their battlefield was the vast Plains of the American West, and they were to ensure the government's plans for **Westward Expansion.**

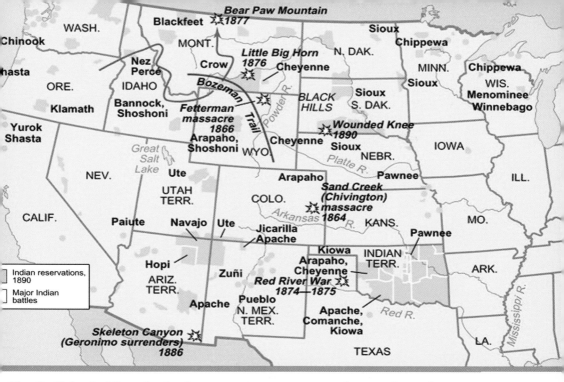

The Buffalo Soldiers had a huge territory to cover during the Indian Wars. They spent most of their time on horseback traveling over the plains, trying to keep the peace.

On one side, spread out across thousands of square miles, were the many Native American peoples, including the Cheyenne (shy-AN), Kiowa (KEE-oh-wah), Comanche (koh-MAN-chee), Apache, Sioux (SOO), and Arapaho (ah-RAH-pah-hoh). These people did not want to give up the land and homes they had known their entire lives, and they were willing to fight to keep them. On the other side of the battle were the many settlers who had flooded into the West searching for a better life—often on that very same land.

Colonel Allen Allensworth was one of the first African American chaplains. He was posted to the 24th Infantry. In 1908, Allensworth established the first black town, located 40 miles outside Bakersfield, California. Through his hard work, the desert wasteland was changed into a thriving pioneer town.

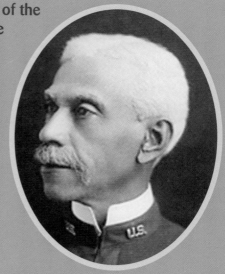

Cathay Williams was a slave during the Civil War. She became the first African American female to enlist as a Buffalo Soldier. She joined the U.S. Army in 1866, disguised as a man and using the name William Cathay. She served for nearly two years.

Into the Wild West

The Buffalo Soldiers, as they would come to be known, came from many backgrounds. They joined for different reasons. Some had fought in the Civil War, and military life was all they knew. Some wanted to enjoy the honor and respect they had never found before in a country that saw them as **inferior** (in-FEE-ree-ur). Others were looking for adventure, eager to journey through a mysterious frontier. Still others only wanted to trade their time and services for food, clothing, shelter, and $13 a month. Most were under twenty years old, and some were not yet sixteen.

Like other soldiers, these troops were taught how to handle horses and weapons. They marched and drilled. Finally, they were sent out West. As peacekeepers, they were to prevent fighting between settlers and Native Americans. In any disagreement, however, they were to defend the settlers.

The soldiers walked and rode throughout thousands of square miles in New Mexico, Arizona, and Texas. They watched to make sure laws were being obeyed. They chased down and captured outlaws who robbed **stagecoaches** or **homesteads.** Other times, the men repaired military posts and built roads and

The 9th and 10th Cavalries, along with the 25th Infantry, were posted in the western barracks at Camp Naco in Cochise County, Texas. The 9th Cavalry was formed in Greenville, Louisiana. The 10th was created in Fort Leavenworth, Kansas. Each regiment had approximately 1,000 men.

One of the Buffalo Soldiers' most important jobs was to guard stagecoaches like this one. Stagecoaches were often threatened by those looking to steal the contents or the horses.

telegraph lines. Throughout it all, they had to cope with the dangers of extreme weather, angry Native Americans, getting lost in the wilderness, and catching illnesses such as **tuberculosis** (too-bur-kyoo-LOH-sis) and **dysentery** (DIH-sen-tayr-ee).

Soon the soldiers earned a nickname from the Native Americans. They were called "buffalo soldiers" because their curly black hair, dark skin, and bravery reminded the Native Americans of the animal. It was a name the soldiers bore with great pride.

The Buffalo Soldiers spent months fighting the Spanish in Cuba. Even though conditions were often challenging, Theodore Roosevelt still described these men as "most gallant and soldierly."

Ignored Heroes

By 1898, the battle for land and control in the West had slowed down. Cuba, an island ninety miles south of Florida, was fighting for independence from Spain. The United States decided to help. The army sent the Buffalo Soldiers to Cuba to fight in the Spanish-American War.

The Buffalo Soldiers traveled to Florida by train. There they met the Rough Riders, a group of inexperienced cowboy fighters. Their leader was future president Theodore Roosevelt. The Buffalo Soldiers and Rough Riders boarded ships, along with their mules, horses, and other supplies. When they finally arrived, they trudged onto the land. They carried rifles and **ammunition** (am-yoo-NIH-shun), plus tents, blankets, and several days' worth of food.

CHAPTER FOUR

One way the soldiers kept safe during battle was to throw hand grenades while hiding behind these shields.

Soon the Buffalo Soldiers were given the chance to show what heroes they were. The Rough Riders were trapped. The Spaniards were shooting, and the cowboys couldn't get to their guns! The mule carrying their weapons had gotten lost. The 10th Cavalry came to the rescue, defeating the Spaniards.

In July, the Buffalo Soldiers proved themselves again in the biggest battle of the war. On San Juan Hill and Kettle Hill, near the city of Santiago, the 9th and 10th Cavalries, along with the Rough Riders, fought the Spaniards. Under the command of Captain John J. "Black Jack" Pershing, they captured the hills and led the troops to victory. The cost was heavy, though. Thousands died, including one out of every five black soldiers who fought.

This painting of the battle at San Juan Hill shows the Buffalo Soldiers as they fought their way closer and closer to the enemy. Although they won, the victory came at a great cost.

The war ended a few weeks later and the soldiers returned to the United States. The Rough Riders were hailed as heroes. Although some reporters wrote about the bravery of the Buffalo Soldiers, **prejudice** (PREH-joo-dis) still existed. In many towns, these brave men could not even walk into a restaurant and sit next to the very same soldiers whose lives they had saved less than a month earlier.

Pancho Villa was a Mexican Revolutionary general. His real name was José Doroteo Arango Arámbula (June 5, 1878 – July 20, 1923).

A World at War

President Woodrow Wilson was upset. The rebel Pancho Villa was causing trouble in Mexico. Wilson had sent American troops over the border to help the Mexican government. Villa and his men wanted control of the country and were not afraid to kill these Americans to win their fight. Wilson turned to "Black Jack" Pershing, who was now a lieutenant, for help.

For the next year, Pershing led the 10th Cavalry over endless miles throughout Mexico. It was not an easy mission. Temperatures soared in the daytime and plummeted at night. Food and supplies ran low. Searching for Pancho Villa was frustrating. He escaped capture again and again. Before he could be caught, the United States faced a bigger problem: World War I (1914–1918).

Buffalo Soldiers work on their aim in France. Although they did not go to the battlefront, their training included rifle practice.

More than 400,000 black soldiers would fight in World War I, although the Buffalo Soldiers did not serve on the front lines. Instead, they were given jobs like taking care of the white soldiers' horses, cooking their food, or repairing their military vehicles. They were treated more like servants than soldiers.

By the time World War II began, black soldiers had gained more respect. In 1936, Benjamin O. Davis Jr. graduated from West Point, the army's officer training college. He would go on to become the first African American Air Force officer to reach the rank of general. His father, Benjamin O. Davis Sr., had been in the 9th Cavalry. In 1940, Davis Sr. became the first African American general in the regular army. When the 99th Fighter **Squadron,** the country's first unit of black fighter pilots, was formed, Davis Jr. was its commander.

With planes in the military, the Buffalo Soldier cavalries were no longer needed.

Some of the descendants of the Buffalo Soldiers became Tuskegee Airmen, the nation's first trained black pilots. These airmen are loading a "baby" or fuel supply tank onto a P-51 Mustang.

Horses were a thing of the past! The men transferred to other units.

Three years after the war ended, President Harry S. Truman signed a bill that ended **segregation** (seh-greh-GAY-shun) in the armed forces. Black soldiers continued to serve in the U.S. military, but they no longer served in separate units.

A monument in Fort Leavenworth, Kansas, honors the service and dedication of the Buffalo Soldiers.

In 1992, a monument was dedicated to the hard work and bravery of the Buffalo Soldiers. A bronze horse carrying a black cavalryman stands at Fort Leavenworth, Kansas, where the 10th Cavalry had been organized in 1867. General Colin Powell was at the groundbreaking ceremony. He was an African American

General Colin Powell

who had risen through the army ranks to become the first black Chairman of the **Joint Chiefs of Staff** for the White House. The statue honoring the Buffalo Soldiers had been his idea. He said at the ceremony, ". . . since 1641 there has never been a time in this country when Blacks were unwilling to serve and sacrifice for America."

Although the Buffalo Soldiers were disbanded more than a half century ago, their legacy will continue for generations. They were brave—both in the line of fire on the battlefields and on the streets when facing prejudice. Their bravery reminds everyone how these men were willing to give their lives for a country that did not even see them as equals.

Congressional Medals of Honor

9th Cavalry Regiment

Captain Francis S. Dodge	Sergeant George Jordan
Second Lieutenant George Burnett	Sergeant Thomas Shaw
Second Lieutenant Mathias W. Day	Sergeant Emanuel Stance
Second Lieutenant Robert T. Emmet	Sergeant Brent Woods
First Sergeant Moses Williams	Corporal Clinton Greaves
Sergeant Thomas Boyne	Corporal William Wilson
Sergeant John Denny	Private Adam Payne
Sergeant Henry Johnson	Private Augustus Walley

10th Cavalry Regiment

Captain Louis Carpenter	Private Dennis Bell
Second Lieutenant Powhatan H. Clarke	Private Fitz Lee
Sergeant Major Edward L. Baker Jr.	Private William Thompkins
Sergeant William McBryar	Private George Wanton

TIMELINE IN HISTORY

1775–1783 The Revolutionary War is fought. At the Boston Massacre on March 5, 1775, five people are killed. One of them, Crispus Attucks, is believed to be of African and Native American descent.

1812–1815 War of 1812; blacks fight in major battles such as the battle of Lake Erie.

1861–1865 The Civil War; 186,000 blacks serve and 33,000 lose their lives.

1865 Congress passes Bill #138, which establishes a peace-time military.

1866–1890 The Buffalo Soldiers are established as part of the U.S. Army.

1880 Buffalo Soldiers under the command of Sergeant George Jordan repulse Victorio and his Apache warriors at Tularosa, New Mexico.

1898 Buffalo Soldiers are sent to Cuba to fight the Spanish-American War; with the Rough Riders, they bring victory at the battle of San Juan and Kettle Hill.

1914–1918 World War I is fought.

1939–1945 World War II is fought.

1940 Benjamin O. Davis Sr. becomes the first African American general in the regular U.S. Army.

1941 The 9th and 10th Cavalry Regiments are combined to form the 4th Cavalry Brigade, commanded by General Benjamin O. Davis Sr.

1941 Tuskegee University begins training the first class of African American military pilots. Its graduates will come to be known as the Tuskegee Airmen.

1942 Benjamin O. Davis Jr. is made commander of the 99th Fighter Squadron.

1944 The horse cavalry regiments are disbanded, ending the era of the Buffalo Soldiers.

1948	President Harry S. Truman signs executive order 9981, which integrates the military.
1950–1953	Korean War is fought; black and white soldiers fight together in the same regiments.
1965–1973	Vietnam War is fought.
1989	General Colin Powell becomes the first African American Chairman of the Joint Chiefs of Staff.
1992	The Buffalo Soldiers monument is dedicated at Fort Leavenworth, Kansas.
2009	African American Barack Obama becomes the 44th president of the United States, making him the first black Commander in Chief of the U.S. military.

FIND OUT MORE

Books

Brouwer, Sigmund. *Great Adventures: Wild Ride, Buffalo Soldier and Other Great Stories.* Carol Stream, IL: Tyndale Kids, 2003.

Flanagan, Alice. *The Buffalo Soldiers.* Minneapolis, MN: Compass Point Books, 2005.

Garland, Sherry. *The Buffalo Soldier.* Gretna, LA: Pelican Publishing Co., 2006.

Glaser, Jason. *Buffalo Soldiers and the American West.* Mankato, Minn.: Capstone Press, 2006.

Hooker, Forrestine. *Child of the Fighting Tenth: On the Frontier with the Buffalo Soldiers.* New York: Oxford University Press, 2003.

Miller, Robert. *Buffalo Soldiers.* East Orange, NJ: Just Us Books, 2005.

FIND OUT MORE

Works Consulted

Desert USA: Buffalo Soldiers
  http://www.desertusa.com/mccain/oct_buffalo.html

Field, Ron. *Buffalo Soldiers 1866–1891.* New York: Osprey
  Publishing, 2005.

———. *Buffalo Soldiers 1892–1918.* New York: Osprey
  Publishing, 2005.

Handbook of Texas Online: Buffalo Soldiers
  http://www.tshaonline.org/handbook/online/articles/BB/
  qlb1.html

Leckie, William H. *The Buffalo Soldiers.* Norman: University of
  Oklahoma Press, 1967.

Schubert, Frank. *Black Valor.* Wilmington, Delaware: Scholarly
  Resources, 1997.

———. *Voices of the Buffalo Soldier.* Albuquerque: University of
  New Mexico Press, 2003.

U.S. Army Center of Military History, Medal of Honor Citations
  http://www.history.army.mil/moh.html

On the Internet

Buffalo Soldiers and Indian Wars
  http://www.buffalosoldier.net/
Buffalo Soldiers National Museum
  http://www.buffalosoldiermuseum.com/
Leavenworth, Kansas: Buffalo Soldier Monument
  http://garrison.leavenworth.army.mil/sites/about/buffalo.asp

GLOSSARY

ammunition (am-yoo-NIH-shun)—Material fired from weapons, such as bombs, bullets, and cannonballs.

cavalry (KAV-ul-ree)—Troops that served on horseback.

community (kuh-MYOO-nih-tee)—A group of people who live together.

detachment (dee-TATCH-ment)—Part of a body of troops sent on a special mission.

dysentery (DIH-sen-tayr-ee)—A disease that causes severe diarrhea.

frontier (frun-TEER)—The border between settled and unsettled areas.

homestead (HOHM-sted)—A dwelling with land and buildings where a family lives.

infantry (IN-fun-tree)—Soldiers who fight on foot.

inferior (in-FEE-ree-ur)—Less than; less valuable or less important.

Joint Chiefs of Staff—The small group of high-ranking officers from the United States military who advise the U.S. government. The Chairman of the Joint Chiefs of Staff is the highest-ranking military officer in the armed forces. This person advises the U.S. President and the Secretary of Defense.

prejudice (PREH-joo-dis)—A negative feeling or opinion about someone based on his or her race, gender, or religion.

quarters (KWOR-ters)—The buildings, houses, or rooms occupied by military personnel and their families.

regiment (REH-juh-munt)—A unit of ground forces, usually made up of two or more units.

segregation (seh-greh-GAY-shun)—The separation of people based on age, gender, or race.

squadron (SKWAH-drun)—A unit of the U.S. Air Force, usually with two or more troops, a headquarters, and supporting units.

stagecoach (STAYJ-kohtch)—An enclosed horse-drawn wagon that traveled over a fixed route with people or cargo.

tuberculosis (tuh-bur-kyoo-LOH-sis)—A disease that affects the lungs.

Westward Expansion (ek-SPAN-shun)—The push during the nineteenth century to move settlers into the western half of North America, land that was occupied primarily by Native Americans.

INDEX